Life in My Garden

A Collection of Haikus and Illustrations

BY LINDA SACEWICZ

©2017 Linda Sacewicz. All Rights Reserved.

ISBN: 978-0-578-19802-6

Dedication

I dedicate this book to my
daughters, Lisa and Laura.
May nature always remain
an important part of your lives.

Introduction

CHOOSING THE RIGHT WORD
IS LIKE PICKING ONE FLOWER
FROM A LARGE BOUQUET.

Table of Contents

MORNING	1
SUMMER RAIN	11
A POTPOURRI OF PLANTS	19
PLANTS A.K.A WEEDS	49
FEATHERED FRIENDS	57
ADDITIONAL COMPANY	67
EVENING	75
NIGHT	81
AUTUMN	87
WINTER	95
WINTER'S FINALE	101

MORNING

Morning

Each morning at four
The birds start singing their song.
Living alarm clocks.

The song of the bird
Sweetly heralds the coming
Of another day.

The darkness of the sky
Is gently broken by dawn.
A pink sliver of light.

Morning

The sun rises.

The city begins to stir.

Sweet overtures of life.

Life in My Garden

In the hot summer
I go outside quite early
To escape the sun.

It's early morning.
Taking my cup of tea
I sit and relax.

Morning

I intend to read
But the book lies unopened.
I rather daydream.

Life in My Garden

The garden is cool
Inviting me to enjoy
Its refreshing calm.

Morning

Squirrels playing tag
Over the fence, up the tree.
Early morning workout.

SUMMER RAIN

Summer Rain

The kiss of soft rain
Lands gently on upturned leaves.
Early morning showers.

A teasing rain leaves
A light coating of moisture
Welcomed by the plants.

The plants are thirsty.
Rain falls, they drink eagerly.
Their leaves rise in joy.

Summer Rain

The rain rushes by
Bathing the rocks with water.
The rocks glisten.

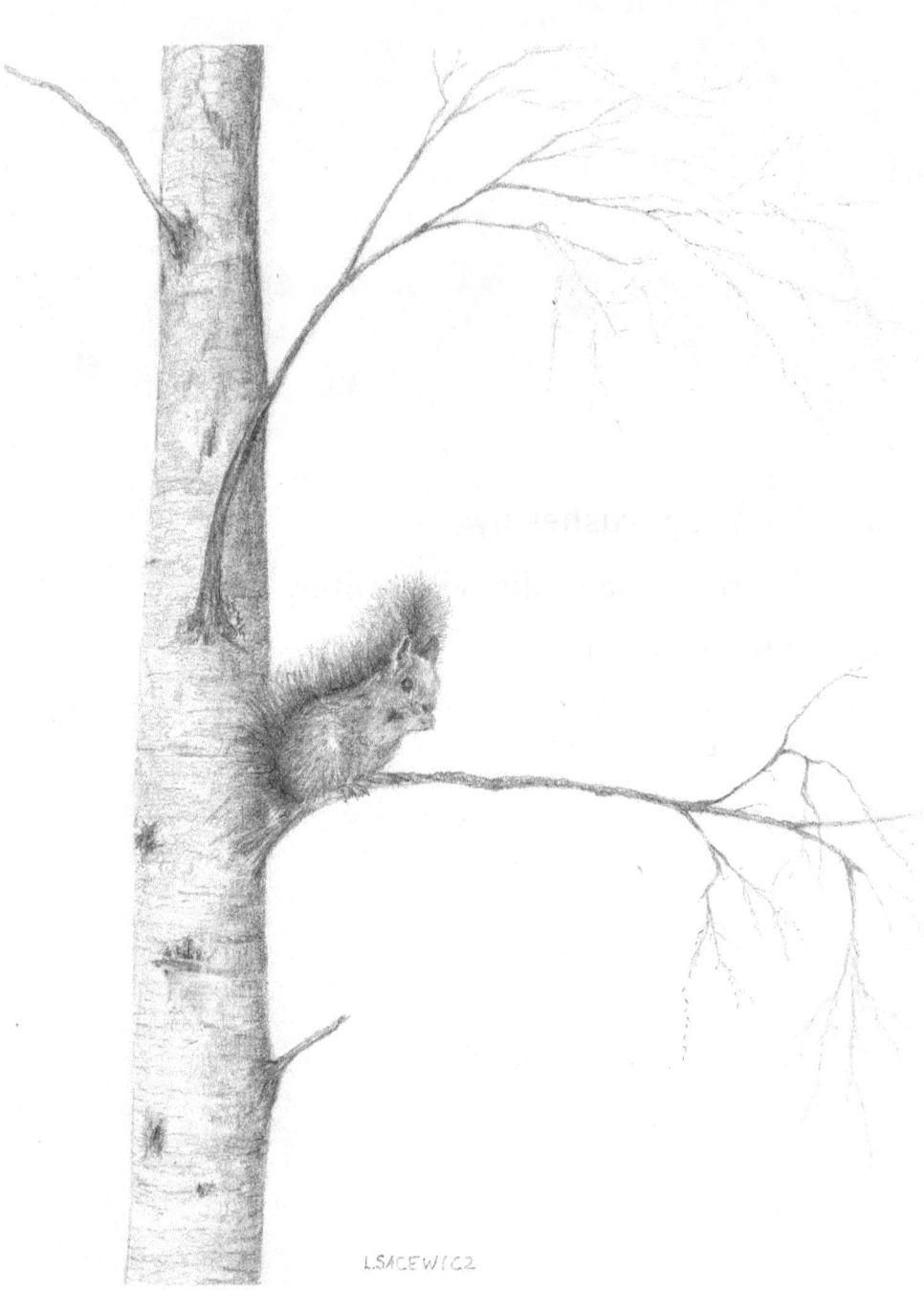

Summer Rain

During the rainstorm
The squirrel lifts its large tail.
Instant umbrella.

The rainbow signals
The end of the sudden storm.
All is well again.

A POTPOURRI OF PLANTS

A Potpourri of Plants

Last night I watered.
The plants look fresh and happy
And so do I.

It is warm outside.

A slight breeze rustles the leaves.

The sound is soothing.

A Potpourri of Plants

Herbs, flowers, green leaves
Co-exist in my garden
In forced harmony.

The plants are swaying
To the tune that they could hear.
Nature's melodies.

Like an orchestra.

Flowers bloom on nature's cue.

Floral symphony.

The stately Lily

Gets ready for its debut.

The garden trumpet.

The Hostas decide
Which one will grow the largest.
They all are winners.

The Hostas leaves spread
Sheltering other plants
Like beach umbrellas.

Within the Hostas
The flowery spikes prepare
For their grand entrance.

Roses in full bloom
Compete against each other
To be the best one.

The mini Rose bush
When given a chance to grow
Is "mini" no more.

The Geraniums
Are always reliable
With their bright colors.

Life in My Garden

The Pansies greet me
With their small cheery faces.
I smile with them too.

The Morning Glories
Won't take "No" for an answer,
Growing where they want.

They hug other plants
Using them to support their ascent
Throughout the garden.

There are annuals
That come up every year
Defying the odds.

Enterprising plants,
Eager to show off their strength
Grow in tiny cracks.

"The tree won't grow tall"
Said the man in the plant store.
It did not listen.

Some plants are rebels.
They do not follow my wishes
Choosing their own space.

The Ivy crawls forth
Densely covering the ground
Like a green leafed snake.

I play "Hide and Seek"
With the long invasive vines.
They hide and I seek.

The creeping Sedum
Spreads at its own steady pace
Setting its own path.

Leaves big and small
Come together in harmony.
My garden carpet.

A Potpourri of Plants

The grapevine stretches
Along the fence with its load
Of green teenaged grapes.

Life in My Garden

The Begonias
Are polite and do not spread.
They stay where planted.

Japanese Maple
Spreads her leafy branches
Like a frilly skirt.

Plants are like children.
Each wanting my attention.
They learn to take turns.

Like a beautician
I cut, trim, shape, and groom
My garden's clients.

The garden and I
Both need daily maintenance
For full potential.

The garden needs me
For regular maintenance.
I need it for peace.

Life in My Garden

The path through the plants
Leads me to a hidden bench.
A place for painting.

My paintbrush in hand,
I try to capture colors.
I succeed, almost.

PLANTS A.K.A WEEDS

Some plants are appalled
Being labeled "Common Weeds".
They try hard to hide.

Life in My Garden

Weeds, flowers, tall grass
Fighting for an empty space
In my small garden.

Plants A.K.A Weeds

If undetected
Weeds can enjoy the benefits
Of my loving care.

Some weeds grow flowers
Trying to prevent their plucking
By the gardener.

The Dandelion
Tried very hard to be loved.
With golden flowers.

We can learn a lot.
Observe how and where weeds grow.
Watch them take chances.

FEATHERED FRIENDS

Feathered Friends

The birds meet to talk
And share the news of the day.
I sit quietly.

From my yard to yours,
They speak to one another.
Bird conversations.

Feathered Friends

The baby Robin
Trying to gain altitude
Flutters his wings.

Life in My Garden

The Mourning Dove comes.
I hear her distinctive sound,
Her rhythmic cooing.

Feathered Friends

She pecks at the ground
Enjoying her early meal.
The breakfast buffet.

The wreath on the door
Becomes a sanctuary
For the baby Doves.

I walk by a nest.
Mother Catbird squawks loudly
Protecting her young.

The birds are hungry.
They reach out from the nest,
Mother obliges.

Feathered Friends

Watch my lawn sprinkler
Create mini mud bath tubs
For the birds to bathe.

ADDITIONAL COMPANY

Life in My Garden

Bumble Bees arrive
Quite early in the morning.
Buzzing company.

The Bee seeks his perch
And climbs into the flower
Enjoying the snack.

Additional Company

A Butterfly comes
As golden as the sun.
A welcomed guest.

Life in My Garden

I saw a Possum.

It was surprised to see me

And scurried away.

Additional Company

The Lady Bug waits.
She wants to be recognized
Unobtrusively.

Ants line up in rows
Practicing their marching skills
For summer picnics.

Life in My Garden

In the tall Birch tree
The squirrel builds her large nest.
Hi-Rise apartment.

The snail creeps forward
Carrying its beige dome.
Portable housing.

Additional Company

Squirrels gamboling,
Busy performing antics.
Free entertainment.

EVENING

Life in My Garden

The evening sky:
Gray, blue, rosy pink, orange
All mingled together.

Evening

The day has ended.
Fireflies come out to play.
Playground for Fairies.

The night time fragrance.
My "Evening in the Bronx"
Honeysuckle blooms.

Life in My Garden

The neighborhood cat
Joins me in the evening,
Silent companion.

The cat finds his bench.
He settles down for the night.
He is my guard cat.

Evening

Once I heard some meows.
The cat returned with a friend
Sharing my garden.

NIGHT

Night

The night sky is clear.
I see a bright shining star
And make two wishes.

I look to the sky
And now see a bright half moon
Adding a faint glow.

Life in My Garden

The birds are quiet.
They find a safe resting place.
Sweet dreams, my dear friends.

It is very dark.
I hate to leave my garden
But I will return.

Night

Night time in silence
Stirs the imagination
Of the day to come.

AUTUMN

Autumn

The days are shorter
A sign that fall is coming.
I enjoy the change.

Leaves dancing carefree
To the music of the wind.
I watch their ballet.

Life in My Garden

Flaming red, gold, bronze
Are the colors of autumn.
They appear overnight.

Autumn

Geese gently gliding
They are soaring to new heights.
All following one.

Life in My Garden

Fall planting of bulbs
Is a vote of confidence.
Spring will come again.

I plant Tulip bulbs.
Half for my springtime pleasure,
Half for the squirrels.

WINTER

Slowly the plants fade
Into the welcoming ground.
Time for a winter's nap.

Winter

Still calm of winter.
The people huddled inside
A time to reflect.

Like Butterfly wings
Looking for a place to land,
Snowflakes are falling.

Icicles hang down
Decorating the tree branch
Like festive jewels.

Snow covers the ground.
I think of what was planted
And what will soon be.

Winter

Snow has stopped falling
And there is a patch of sun.
I sit in its warmth.

WINTER'S FINALE

Winter's Finale

Crocus are welcomed.
"How good to see you, at last"
Winter was so long.

The flowers peek out
From their melting snow blanket.
Spring is coming soon.

And so the cycles of nature continue.

LEAVE SOME EMPTY SPOTS
IN YOUR GARDEN AND YOUR LIFE
AWAITING THE UNKNOWN.

www.ingramcontent.com/pod-product-compliance
Lightning Source LLC
Chambersburg PA
CBHW061450040426
42450CB00007B/1293